Up On Big Rock Poetry Series
SHIPWRECKT BOOKS PUBLISHING COMPANY
Winona, Minnesota

Other books by Mara Adamitz Scrupe

"In the Bare Bones House of Was: Poems,"
Brighthorse Books

"Eat the Marrow," erbacce-press, London

"Beast," National Federation of State Poetry Societies Press

Reap

a Flora

Mara
Adamitz
Scrupe

Original botanical drawings cover and interior by the author.
Cover and interior format by Shipwreckt Books.

Shipwreckt Books Publishing Company
357 W. Wabasha St.
Winona, Minnesota, 55987

Library of Congress Control Number: 2023930181

ISBN: 979-8-9875338-1-9

For all the insistent, unyielding makers and caretakers.

Contents

i. Pontederia cordata/ Pickerelweed

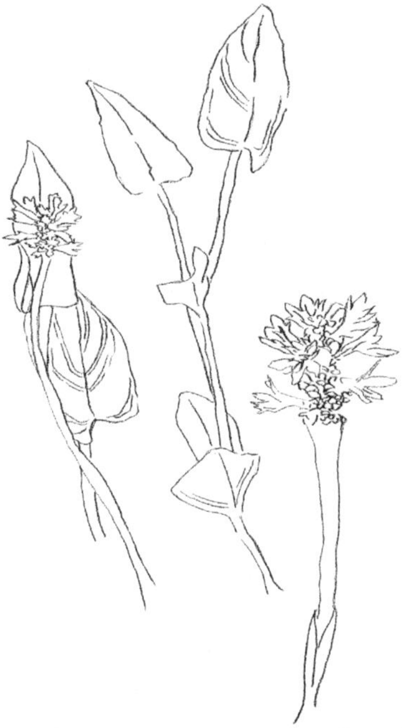

you have a dream the kind of dream

you completely believe

emergent of bees' fulvid
flowerings/ you're back-float cataract

soothe bay & fluctuate/ bent

& submergent
dispersed & buried hermetic

as hidden awaiting inception

menisci of tenderness

it was mid-December the first time
we saw Saturn
& all the slaves became masters & the children   adults
& the seeds still wore their burrowing coats
scored soft
suffering toward spring   & daybreak stretched
across the valley & ice hulls hobbled
seesawing downstream & the tree line I've memorized
dematerialized in an inversion after last night's

warm rain   a coral flush a boost of thin cobalt splay

east to west & lying here I thought
which is peace & which
death
we listened to the rill of heat coils under brick floors
we recalled daffodils
at the bus stop bunched in old ladies' broad
fists & a creature's resistance
to turning   *turning*
& a lair not a flame a ring lingering or a line
taken   & redress keeping place

our holding/ our plot/ the yolky beaded

necklace on a temporary string the root
& spray   we bought in a Baltic town
the reach & draw the straddle
of ancient oaks & resurrection
what we expect what we anticipate

when the charlatan leads the prayer when dirt
flowers the promise of a better world
when gold sheaf & a tired Russian idol an image of virgin
& child   goes grace   & frill rubs young for us

again frost & fuss & the menisci of tenderness

curve up/ the threadbare tension the rend & scratch
of muscle against bone & I wonder which delights
we let slip on our journeys which foods
& spirits   parcels & lands bogs & fens
which breathing spawn & multitudes hung comatose
            waiting on our mortal spell: the camera's eye
flashback to an old idea: a small world spinning
gamboling animatrons in micromotion/ gleeful
            gorgeous optimism
scarified ovum   sprouting

Sfumato

that was our summer of glorious ripe   of bright
painted cottages & cottagers
dabbing touch-ups
of burnished midnights & endless
cups of coffee

that summer
in which near alpine
birds descended on blur-edged wings   their contours
rendered softly as they appeared
from a distance to naked eyes   that summer

of pageants & spectacles
meant to dissipate our discontent
in tears & heat obscurant
that summer of alluring girls lounged
on angel-built precipices on pierced

palisades our pink pulp stretched
to haze –
that summer as vigilantes stacked
secluded in fjords indistinct
across the vale in equivalents of painterly

sfumato illusions of death & sex
& innocence & intimacy – rudimentary
as dry wash   & conté
-mapped –   in our enigmatic smiles & eyes
that summer we busted out

labially/ blushed
ruddy in corseted
allusions – such profusions –
that summer of berserker solstice
bonfires burning close explicit & clear

Purple Spear Thistle

as mystery's lure
as burrow sprung's clench fixed as shadow
as millenary heritor born & reborn again

& again I'm agency's skeptic playing
the odds/ essential yield/ peak or gain a particle
profane & sacred of the sanctified

undivine stinking of onion grass & saltwater
twang of spring-thawed manure I lie whole
& heavy side by side eighty-five thousand

exhumed Buddhic bones/ divided/ a parietal slope
among the linen-bound & bundled swaddled
hoard/ coped & scraped/ an iron-lined

stone dollhouse stupa cradling a silver-bracted
sandalwood case living heavy living
light as commonplace an ancestor as workaday

a wheel spinning flax bast to thread
a runner of ivory ecru of patterned
damask luster cut & doled out in

twelve equal pieces one for each of me of them
of those yet unborn yet unreleased
afloat adrift tacking the shiftless night sky's

alignments/ I am that spinner's pedigree that
maker's blood cells vigilant in my own her DNA
observant in mine discipled or indifferent

blunt & fine prophet of heretical aberrations & bio-
neurological treason's auspicious hemocytic
minglings as apostle of impossibilities

of surprise of unleashed of rising up gloam or glare
but I am too autonomy's insistence
fleeing blood bond's lead shot across our homestead's

untrod barrens its teeming tracts/ mugwort marsh
reed & bristle purple spear thistle's
ornery outside prickle/ creamy inside pulp

in solstice

                    in first light's cirrostratus flush/ cumulous
bloom unbound/ in halo
Earth stood heaven's bitter blast

          trembled leaden slaps

& in great sweltering pluralities in sidereal
          midnights we fixed our starry
          stars stretched out
          in leniency's allowance in solstice's lustered

dimmet/ we shored our nostalgia our breakfast cakes
& jams   reminded that what we do iteratively

          this world reiterates

we saw ourselves in flash & flare qualms & scruples
seduced by Northern Lights/ repentant raw
drunks knocked sober   forfeit
          lost & found/ *that* primrose path we soft-

skidded sideways we drifted/ bumped up
against the guardrail

          it never snows so hard as in a single Sunday's scud
          & lift lake's azure lapping as we wake in yarrow

in Queen Anne's Lace or in your case in Stork's Bill's
          restraint as roadside wearies we kept

the fiery stir   blinded by the yellow of the sky
kept on shining in our black woolen suits

& yes in the house where we slept it was cold
but outside cafés buzzed streets binged & tipsy
shot the moon

in spring melt's icy hiems husk we plunged in bees' butter
sweet tooth sap   sticky chunk to wild
smooth comb & syrupy splint

scooped straight out from a Mason jar

we dug in our holes twice as wide as deep
– a fork full of bone meal –
never plant a new one where an old one dies

we climbed the loon's cry/ the harrow/ our bodies'
humming   compared in light in turquoise stroke
& mendicants' sighs

late-summer's naked slant

sleepless anchored/ in bister span our boats'
survey/ our crest & surge

so fast *so fast*

we made in poppy's reckless
blaze   appetites/ respite
our gaze the glittery filthy streets   ah beauty *beauty*

begs   in clement spent in caution's
lean return   in winter's
recuperative slip   we made our amends

eyas

some come reeling salty chirr-slick
        to life   or moated
        linger/ submerged & abeyant
        but before we know it – flesh-flecked

in afterbirth –

we're ankle/ calf/ knee deep/ thigh high in lap
& swell/ mortal torrent/ aqueous
        & afire all action & reaction & no stops

in between/ ungovernable
some look down crank the wheel off-
bridge & fly/ reverberant or silent – dive & crash –
some gust flood-rocked

        – as the ocean throbs & gives   as the gathering
crowd chants – *come in little refugee*
welcome –

//

a cradle tied with twine to the wall sconce torn
        from its socket/ rocking   *rocking*

the lane-side-mother-swat countervails
        the gutter slide/ rough spots

– toughed out & tamed in tears of creamy unguent
raw as the unripe
crown of a newborn's head –

tracked & checked & carefully polished/ you know
some paddle easy
through this world & some come tempest-
stung beseeching universal

mercy or gratefully eagerly fleetingly in recalibration
of all things calculable

– two equal sides of a saddlebag house
dogtrot
in between a little kid's immaculateness
& a grown-up's ramshackle sediment & debris –

sidestepped sidled or straddled tiptoed
or tramping/ my forked sticks clutched/ my twigs
crossed
& shivering I try divining that unsullied

underground spring/ the celadon march/ reverie
in spiraling blueprints of abstraction

//

a red-tailed hawk with her two times the power
of human sight drifts drafting/ slows
her breakneck fastest on earth velocity eyes
the hooded-in-harness captive-in-training tutored
wild mold to kill

as that nestling jerks its jesses
swerves &

//

– the child's always the prize watching
the slaughter learning the process
by heart something
to keep in mind –

stalked & slain & field-dressed in ecumenical
conundrum – be the eater
or the eaten – elucidation

by immersion at the canvas-covered
kitchen table/ break the legs at the elbows/ save the heart
the liver the lungs for last

ii. Antennaria plantaginifolia/ Pussy Toes

is the pale

beyond the viridarium   the hot house

thrall in smallish praise to lowly

the rest boast & overmuch
immodest

bounded/ roadside cat's paw
downy pad/ tiny albino/ almost
ambulant

as though stirred   to tremble

Imago & the Io Moth

in a single metamorphosis
also known alluringly as the *imaginal* state
or ingloriously as grown/ adult

or in multitudes: *imagines*

in fire-wing greens & pink furl & forests' tastings breed
the tinnish bracken on our tongues
the sap of storm-strike
the brood of copper zipper

heat lightening: spring's lasering in on iron weed's
drive in bursts & clusters/ lavender
progeniture/ profusions beside the dying Magnolia

remind me of your passing
in September   in Dogwood's leaflitter
& Maple blaze the Io lays her eggs/ a larval hatch

marching & feeding down the silk line
queueing on rosettes of drowsy
facing outward/ protected
by spiny stingers/ inflammatory then dormant
for the molted sleep I'm alone

for all my unslept days & nights   I'm mute
for all the gregariousness
of our veins' orbiting in a single
blinking Mason jar's

unfolding in manuscripts of velvety pigments'
brilliance: our favorite Titian Peale's categoric
accuracy/ emergent/ we were heads-down

hiding or secure in scientific distance
                                    or winged in dreamt flight: I dreamt

the dream of not being alone
& yet again & for our only time: *imago*: our childhood
covert in a Minnesota cornfield   renegade
                  & redefined we dreamt our self-made asylum

they'd never find us hidden within & sure
wrapped without
consumed in alcoholic chaos/ tears & blur

                  & covering for him framed our normal: as the Io
goes so go the unguarded calmed & trussed
children certain closed-eyed of their
invisibility of unspoken

culpability cocooned in denial then thrust
                  against the crash   ousted in purparial shuck
                  like it or not tragic & matter of fact
we welcomed the brand new everyday of our
old unfolding

what would be his apology
or apogee: climax & dissolution/ division
in startle position
                    – by contrast the Io only lives a single week –

each bloom-lashed rear wing's staring eyespot's
crackerjack cover against the predator
        the nearly perfect palliative
        or hindmost defense

Balsam/ sister sister

in faint – branchlet's pricklings against our palms –
in pungent & silvery-tipped   poked
& stranded threads against bare feet in spice-
scented darkness   half-drunk as goddesses
we dreamt ourselves up

in lanterns' absence we shined imagined windows
in aesthetic consolation row upon row   *dear God*
how we shone   sister *sister* spirally on the shoot

in slight in serrated pinked push against calves
at frond's edge   tickled & blooded & groped
we claimed our time in pure madness of being
alive

or much later/ older/ saner in shady stippled light sole
& satisfied for the makings of our hands
in crucibles' forged hacksilver in millefiori beads
cut from molten cullet   we covered our nakedness

with tesserae sharps sandwiched shining in gold foil
like our mothers' mothers evergreen was our first best

choice   afloat as resin's balm as unguent &
poultice for sting & outrage (the old man's
pollens released)

we moved in remembered dreams our bodily
incense stoked the viewing we birthed beatae

in our crevasses   *O the balsam*

musk marked us rich beyond knowing
unfathomed in our wealth
pressed & balanced our toes & fingers claimed cold

slate slabs without chancel or stained-glass partitions
to protect us   flying   falling

            sister *sister* we kept

still beyond prayer & piety – paternal
rage on a drunk – we waited grasping the margins' lean
embrace (pledged muscles
to breasts/ whittled bones from our hearts

& lungs) we toughed it out in some rare
            collaboration some
fragile environ or ecosystem/ hunched inebriate

shimmerings/ shameless dusk-coming roseate
too delicate to amplify passed through our eyes into
our bodies' rough & fissured kicked by Dad
            out from under our beds

(for once we knew just how to behave
            if we could only get out of the way)
                                                            & in intervals
of vested/ needled thickly as sheltered/ halfway
hidden we vaulted/ careering   (certainly)
                        but ascended/ unbroken

dupy: plural of *dupa* Polish for ass

a birder's cacophony/ kettle lake & moraine

their whole lives deer walk tippy toed
as though on eggshells
          reluctant to rut-in much of a trail
attentive
but diffident in the same season when tracking is easiest

we built cold forts with our bare hands
just to get out
when it's most difficult telling one strain
          from another
sorting snow our noses up-tilted snuffling
the ice-sterile breeze our stubby paws bitter-

          whitened then blued
we were lost & found for burrowed
in our doggy anatomy our pooch-y pad
          in our cuddling
unfathomable as though structure constrained
          is no ease at all   *a home*

          we called it   *safe*   the world's rock face
compared us/ our family unfavorably
inside to outside   contrast to conformity
we came as triad
          my twofold sisters & I years later

spatial memory left us disconnected

& rambling
    our littler bodies' contiguous grasp
once contained in a homemade igloo
& a handful of pennies that showed up
    silvery as snowballs
in my five-year-old's intestines

I shat them out – you both made me remember that –
    Mom dug for them
just to make sure which strangely
    makes me think of Dad
who so loved creatures
& the glasshouse trap he built for fitting
    for him to look out

observing understanding calculating
    yet untouched   nor touching
banging against the glass
    we never came much closer
we sure as hell got off our *dupy*
    huddled in the corner
under the bed   frozen in darkness's fitful quell

    we could have roused one another
had we known
or dared our hands' unfolding
    we should have tossed ourselves
up in the air & flown as Black-capped Chickadees
& House Sparrows skinny little finches
    or plain Pine Siskins when heavy weather came

as it always did – just another inebriant north

of predictable northern vices –
mobbing the feeder in the same imperfect
    overwintering respite
we forgot to oppose as opposing females
    sisters after all
awakened instead to decades past/ years later

by the loudest birds you ever heard
a common Carolina Wrens' cacophony
in the indolence of rudimentary time
    of boreal redound /the land's glacial
rise our sinking/ kettle lake & moraine
         drunk & sober
 appellate & reconciled in amnesty's incense:

in the sea scent of southern littoral

    so far from raw   from our wintry start
    from childhood's shaky pitch
temperance/ his terrible thin veneer
& the improbability
of here & now   missing him

Anamnesis/ in the absence of light

& in my real life   all my windows
have screens but here when the sounds

of the day's night fly to the ceiling   up & creep
to the floor   down   over nub-budded

branches dark/ legs glistening   anamnesis
crawls into my mouth & my father sliding the rose

gold & onyx ring from his finger to mine the meat
of my thumb worrying the stone's chipped facet

his sorrow's *shift*   his grief's *transference*
& in my real life I talk to anyone who wags

his tail to get a treat but here *here* I speak
only to cows sheep horses mules donkeys barren

hinnies & jacks high as stallions I stand
clear/ hoary close winter's coats sure unshod

hooves sunk in miry slush   & in this real
life I'm villein enthralled the land my body's

captive toil I'm against proportion beautifully
imperfect torque/ imbalance thrills me   *thrilled*

I'm off on a viking   a medieval seeker
on my couch in a cab/ white underbelly of squirrels

my cloak guardians/ tokens/ piss unguent & sea
balm I'm traveler unmoored/ the gemstone's

blind the fetish's jagged precipice/ invisible as
black in the absence of light.

Drawing the Sacred Dog

in feedlots of lambs & calves & piglets I look
for dominant/ frightless/ the hip to shoulder length
of a beast's body measured in the distance between

its prints in orange-feathered
blackness in the stain of economical red/ blooded
rimming verdure/ brooding ghosts circulate prey

tracking what sort of animal
ambles unhurried through the chute which raptor hits
& drags fighting in the snow marking

in its stertor its stridor the narrowing
or blockage of airways in the gist in magnificence
the sacred dog/ in spent I look for ordered/ defensive

in the splendor/ symmetry in the ardor & clamber
the scramble in the daily holy battle unmurdered/ the kill
the living unmediated by sprawl or density or bipedal

mercy on a soft moss path I look for whole
not differentiated heart-shaped deer hooves' dew claws
impressed crisscrossing the perspectival/ the bolt blow

to the head/ rendering an illusion of shading
from flatness to roundness drawing the form of human
the most fragile of species/ the most especially

encumbered

iii. Monarda didyma/ American Beebalm

adorn me take of me my
body/ paradeisos from the Persian *pardes:*

of paradise adore me/ heathenish

of bent & glassy slopes I'm fallen of
clung & charted/ bypassed or dead-headed

I'll come again &

again pluck & replant me I'll recover

sanguine/ colonial/ random & rash
& new-coursed
or tranquil as tea & languish

Milfoil

in a box pew in the partisan's temple/ earthed over
under ground
I am the quiet one speaking endurance/ compassion

in the unendurable in the agre-dulce bitter
-sweetness sleet's

remorselessness stinging   & since you ask
it's getting cold here going down below freezing
tonight possibly flurries   blanketed/ surrounded
at the warm barrel stove set solid/ black oil
smudge summer-lost dust-draped

          tables & chairs
          & chests of drawers

in wintry ice crust wood wax susurration   *slide*
in diglossia/ the use of two languages to cast as one:
          pain & pleasure snare & truss snatch &
shuck/ birch bark brush my neck could have snapped

          just like

in the adolescents' bethel in the basement
in the marriage of spur & widows' haunches
keeled Stations of the Cross disciples carved
on every lintel slip beneath raw frost-bound

voracious of unrefined of ideologies
& romancers & shut-ins like me wheelbarrows'

snow-soundlessness under silk pack & harness'
spread unwound in shape in light the things
that comfort us: green-walled roads/ gem-celled
vivaries/ our beasts safe asleep in emergency

bivouac   my arms cast in pearly outskirts
the last of the butterfly weed post
-cutworm swarm & swallow our first sex

O   *O*

& in the tourist temple Milfoil choke chokes
the Chains past lake's
rough & cabin's north/ November's envoy *absit*
omen: in that wriggling black sack
we fished out   from the trash

Bindweed

how the birds came to sing
even how we named them – such departures squalls

& torrents –

a titmouse scurried across the lane fast
& unforeseen & the rural carrier

flew past with a wave
& a shout & a long-legged

hare galumphed
out of sight   & bindweed & wild

raspberries smelled the rain

before it came

Reliquiae Flyway

starting with the thumbnail heart nut
gather of splinter wood
fungus of soft rot
she lays out her tools of dissection

scalpel-fitted blades/ 12's & 20's
forceps & curved scissors squared
on her diagram:
she's routing the long Atlantic Flyway

supposing we are all saltwater
cloudburst's accretions collected
gully-washers tasting of tin
figment quickened rivulets she considers

reversing death to birth foul
to pure bodies down-breathed/ marsh sedge
turned mud-plaster & razor
-edge *considering*

she thinks we are each
our own reach stretched to capture
graced or graceless amen *amen* succored
amen in this high making

back to life amen amen
as though fine & potent she translates flight
to her fingers she wonders
what can it mean to translate

word for word movement
for movement &
if she wanted could she dart & sail & dive
stumble the root-caved walk/ plucked/ fallen/ feeling

reflexively its motility its pains &
pleasures with it for it
recalling its qualms & resistance & blessings
she makes herself over

allies herself forever with Fox Sparrow
against albatross's & cormorant's & heron's
amaranthine appetites/ boned wing bars endemic
or not/ Horus the bird-head's dust

spun upward not braced & chamfered
polished sheeny in fetch & mount & accumulate &
display but street birds trusting
the first hunch/ amen/ skeptics' cold cored

guts/ clean sheeting/ vestigial/ piled
unwashed unenbalmed her moss-filled body
sewn bright & tight/ warmth in fervent triple-
stranded embroidery/ avid cottons & silks

amen she sees herself sutured
in white-work bird breast stuffed &
padded patterned dog star & fern couched
in long & satin stitches

French knots & touch-me-not thistles

in cobweb markings preserved
            by convent sisters proud enough not to want
to disappear   she considers herself an artist

                        of innuendo she imagines
praise in her flight – flushed & febrile – the sort that
only comes with experience
                        passementeries

                        shrublands & woodlands & wetlands
& millions on land on foot looking up stunned
en masse congregants
fledged   of this fragile coastline

Judas Hole

After the warnings we could have
gotten through it
        in remonstrance steam gatherers rose
in terrorem
        each with give & fine devilish

strokes/ swoozy/ in black slip & bruise-mottled
        a shrike
        harsh & passerine sang & sued & spiked a lubber
grasshopper & let the poison drop

to obsolete/ the longer gone the settler
the goner got   a thew scrap impaled & tore the flesh
        or cached it for later   & blind

the dogs of night shot for bother   for hindrance
        & spark
ignited the powder too near to the party well

        underway & we drank to life
& death & considered it spoken in quinoctial thirst
        cicadas shrieked
        & warriors shirred

& starred our songbird's materials & fabric
        with matériel of force a certain war
        for keep & refuge

for survival in that famous parkland of European
bison hunted to near extinction & in a future we defined

as something
personal/ pointed/ human/ & the wild as something
unfamilial in the exterminator's
the adventurer's the hunter's clean & priestly

rapids we replaced
the living animals (so difficult
to keep) with stuffed reminders/ marsh toad
& turnstile

& in that great chain of being/ tensile in drifts
& storms & in our ruthless human

hordes/ carnivorous
omnivorous/ & in our cunning & in our impotent
rage against the universal hubris we sited

through the Judas hole of avarice
the last specimen shot
in Białowieża forest

Mine

Rose the first so I named her. How I
found her shivering tick-tumid hide
in high pasture   how she
died in my arms. How we buried her
in a hand-planed hinged box.

Toy tatted puppy mill poodle. Pink-eared.
Translucent. How he wouldn't hold
close how I couldn't calm his tiny
struggling
self.

Hurtling hound on the highway. How I
pulled over ajar door dinging. Grabbed
her.   Bloody-nippled raw. How she lay
her head in my lap as I drove.
How I stroked her paw.

How I learned. Ferals don't
tame down. For months
I brought food. Water. How they
never let me
near.

Dropped off brood. Farm
gate to the highway.
Squirming balls. Flesh & fur.
How their eyes opened
almost.

I can show you   out back.
In the herb bed. Beside the old
summer kitchen. The soil
caved in a little. The shapes of small
rectangles.

The Tracker's Tale

only say a name for the mammal's trace/ for amplitude
say *noiseless* or *sound*   ordinary
          blessings/ say the compass's
periphery: oath on oath spine on spine the young
born hairless

& blind   at arm's-length   wind-shorn or sylvan
say a word for   *habit* or *instinct*
          full possessors of clouds & sky & sun
          & in footprints indistinct in limbered

fields or decipherable after the squall in spill's
darkness in saltwater
patterns made before the light
before miracles & simples emollients & concoctions

          say a name   one each
          for *badger*   & *rabbit*
          for hare's progress
          crossing tundra flats

or the skunk holed-up in the crawl space
under my floorboards

          say as many words as you can think of
          for snowy glint of river returning to winter

the tracker's tale/ the linguist's lesson tell
in any proper parlance you choose/ snowdrifts

are *fingers*   or *penitents' spikes*   say
signing in hands: my thighs my calves
my piedmont powerful toes/ muscled to tour
to trek & prowl/ prepared

for the long haul
          in forest scour & varnished blight/ unsheltered
          say a name   one each
          for *coyote*   *bear* &   *bobcat*

suicides forced off the cliff
by the documentary camera crew
count them up collected: scats identified by riddled
contents of stomachs & intestines/ that spring's
unfolding

          in the pipeline & the clear cut/ forced exodus

          coyote black bear & bobcat

& our moorings/ mice ribs in the barn struts owls'
          droppings/ cottontail
          tuft in the coy-dog dung

make sense in words of corporeal warnings/ describe
with drawings the front vestigial anteriorly bi-lobed toe
          diagnostic of a wild cat print summed up
          in the single Siberian swan
          settling in   one foot tucked
          atop her back/ palliate/ the other paddling manic
below

talk the same as foolish fire
& blessed *blessed*
with abundance/ add back-scratch & worktop
covered in dents
scorched & finished in rose blood
ransom & reckoning

iv. Sarracenia purpurea/Purple Pitcher Plant

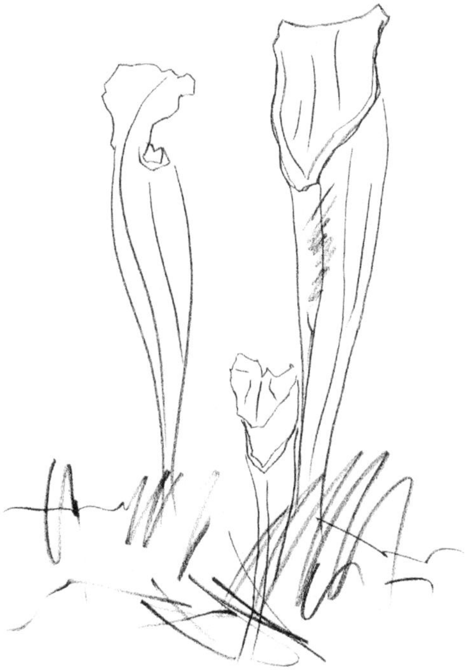

essence or sepulcher/ traipsing
gallivanting

fraternization
or a marriage

of trap & entente/ prey & pitcher

drowned in freshwater pulpy testicles'
collection or commensal

meaning sharing
the same table

The Sea Between Us

I'm a stowaway   a song before sound
an explorer a collector/ assignee of old
world seeds set afloat
in hinged wooden boxes

latched/ thrown overboard as cyclonic
reminder   reparation   repatriation my flora
an inventor's design a pirate's bounty

graftings cleave my barbarian brain/ forced
hothouse swells   my gorgeous sumptuous monstrous
artificialities/ hybridities as false as Fairchild's

Mule sexing Sweet William & common pink a breeder's
imperfect universe/ inosculation
jointed crossings   vascular eventualities
bled one into another

ray to atom speck to shred
to trickle/ underground & blind
like everyone I admire what's shaped
in my likeness   I'm a maze set free

absolved of botany's sin of playing God
I've managed to stay upright in this shit
storm world dream myself beyond me

at a distance far greater
than my body's reach or substance   ocean to
freshwater to inland sea I've kept fast to

my bailey/ Martello/ Cork coast or Halifax
passage   I pick my blossoms past their
prime/ roses' rot scent tokens nuts & berries
scooped on my tongue stuffed in my cheeks

you ask   *you*   corralled at my kitchen table
refusing the food I set before   you you *you* won't

eat with me but sing your songs into my teeth
yes & breasts & spine   your language
a croon a lullaby a torrent you slip into my bath
rocks & raffia

sweet apple alien   our coffees cooling   you
you argue   bliss/ the possibilities
of surrender
of ecstasy   *all in favor*   *of?*   while

I caution acquiescence: that which is   *is*
after all & can can only be   *be*
as the parts assuage
the whole the rootstock the scion

which one was I/ and which were you?
kept somehow
alive while our tissues made contact our veinous
cambia connected   yet graft our frailest

axis: do I still love? you ask me   odd
it seems   so so immaterial   I demur:
don't you?   but let's let that
go for now let's

wander other paths   make patience
our garden track high the hot
sun's straight overhead pulling us up
up

upright/ maybe rapture's
beside the point   or as close as we'll come
to our dying or perhaps our tempests

in their unyielding their resistance gentle us
habituate heal & bind us strongest
at our weakest conjoint

Taproot

It's rowboats slapping when the wind kicks up
            keeps me calm

It's Dow Chemical's pink plant glow passed slow
along the CSX tracks   if it's tree

I choose dwarf   rough & crippled
            Prunus/ slight nursed looking

Thing   if it's stab my veins eight digs deep
            amaranth ream/ it's metaphysics

            gnawing   *gnawing*

I knock my knuckles against the wall pearls
            fall   I gather them up   if it's taper

Thick   & snout down dominant
it's digging from which all others sprout/ a living

Plough a columnar shaft   a sweet swelling
            out from the base

            & back again to the capital/ volcanic

Menhir   vesicular granite/ one takes root
            while the other mounts

            budding   burgeoning

If we should be blessed by some great reward, it's the fruit of a seed planted by us in the past.
- *Bodhidharma*

despite & obviously & after all

please

let me off easy & let's not
separate but by our own limits & legends
live we wedded pair we milestone planted
pears: in our maturity/ endurance/ our strength
& if in the infinite
weal that welds us each has only one lesson
to learn & relearn
then you *you* are the bull's blood of our
mortar the river rock hearth the fired

furnace to my lightning strike/ my peal
rends the night but you're the carved knight's
stone feet resting eternally
on a dog's back you bare-balled
& soaking wet pulling the cushions in
from the storm you rod repairman
the one that keeps falling on my head every time
I draw the curtains *you*
jack of all trades you master of many you cleated
tree climber in cutoff shorts & wife-beater tee
block & tackle shinny out on a limb you

as alert to pitch as I am to trussed
& released dabbler heliocentrist that I am you put me
to shame you make round earth
your center poor backwoods pilgrim that I am

you make me grin have a beer
we are only here a short time so mill the barley
mix the mash part the wort from spent grain

I'm flame/ you: fermentation let's boil it down:
fights & failings & faith & if all
we amount to is just so many worthless
trinkets – no flying flags or finery –
our very skins might just shed us quick
as a lick & off they'd go in the altogether
nothing left behind but scraps & guts
slack/ status
undefined just our human hurts &
hearts hemorrhaged one into the other

after Corot in love

amaranthine stain/ lilac blooms
          bled & kind   brindled
          in a raven's dream in a lark's lesson flown
in civilized voice that reason

belies how splendid but fraught the underbelly
this upside-down paean
plum blossom & cherry fruit scattered

in our wildness

          we swept away those pink petals
          how confusingly baroque
trying to find a chink a hollow a place

in lying love
in so much darkness to catch the light/ mind
the lullaby of twilit skies   & purplish

—

we soothed & trembled rocks & shelves
          we converged heat-heightened drifting

& at the southern terminus aquamarine fields'
tallow pitch & coal dust   we too read

beneath the trees   we two in a queen's
bed   head-planks of dragons' beards &
bric-a-brac amassed in reds & yellows/ orange-carved
the mast of our elegant ship/ cantata:

restraint & recitative
ornament & continuo
rewards & rocking
rapture & dissonance

———

rabbit-fur-laced coyote scat marked that species'
profound defense   forest breach & clear cut

bisected by our lane
left for us to come upon   the morning after

the horologist's gift

according to a pattern or habit a method
or the genius of deficiency/ a gift all his own
& not necessarily
a particularity or imprecision of his body
& blood (though he prays he always
has) but truly as vexatious & miraculous as heaven's

own healing in the sleight-of-hand of a milkmaid's casual
pestilential resistance or truly as hollow
as the tock-tock TOCK of his multiple mantle
clocks/ ruthless reminders
of unrecalled or stilled or simply lost still
instinctively he bares their backs/ fiddles their works

keys & mainsprings &
gears

weights &
pendulums

he listens hard for the healing as though the secret's
revealed right there in front of him

& together they calculate each timepiece's merits

& the stranger swears they've found a good home

a commoner bird/ a redbird out the window
chants
          concertizing in time & rhythm
& in his bewildered expertise & occasional
outrage
– he will thunder as the blind man preaches –
          the horologist checks & balances
& memoryless finesses for useful record
          the practical parts that only his hands remember

River

It's a river into which each must dip
a paddle swing an oar plant a pole &
          push off
you can only stay upright ahead
of the current/ control is a giddy fiction
in a blow-up raft   audacity's
smooth arms & legs companionably
tangled
lounged in bulging black inner tubes spun
guileless or sure in a two-man canoe
or lone but quick
          in a kayak you must each one
slide in the day is bright even brisk & brown-clouded
          red from spring's deluge you think you'll know
what to avoid how to bypass boulders rising
to block your way/ too fast   you won't be certain which
way to go left or right & anyway it doesn't
matter   take your pick   lean to the left & pull hard
on the paddle – I want to tell you – what you see may
only be the topmost threat   worse lies beneath
          the waterline   waiting
to upend you   to deflate & drown you
the timid the bold the careless the joyous.
Now I've come with you as far as I can
& like the mother I'll never be I know to let
          go the rope
I'll steer toward the shallows swinging both
feet over the side/ cautiously stepping out thigh-
          high in the grasp/ it wants to carry
me along with you   but I've made this trip

before now it's your turn/ left arm outstretched
for balance toes feeling gingerly
for bottom for smooth & solid stones
with my right hand I'll haul my boat
against the rush   to the calmed
all the while twisting in the
flow   I'll squint
to watch you dissolve dark &
indistinguishable
from trees bordering land
I'll make for a sandbar   &
trepidation:
Did I give you the proper charts   the maps?
Have I warned you the warnings you'll need the most?
Test water's depth with length of oar.
Straighten up in drought & haul
            yourself to shore.

v. Symplocarpus foetidus/ Skunk Cabbage

spathe-cradled spadix/ carrion
voodoo/ profligate

perfume: licentious: self-emenant flux &

hot sex on the fly
thermogenesis & metasis

carpus/my twisted arthritic wrist's

root-cooked cartilaginous deep-ice
cure/ salve the purplish stench

of blisterish/ of tongued & bumbled fetor

the age of drift

did you mean icy rivers of crystalline flow or fossil
pallets over bedrock or alluvial shock: shifted boulder
clay or did you have in mind the shallow/ tittle-
marked & prettily painted fragment/ an aspirant's indicia
or paternal/ rude stone weapons

incised with a stag's or a rhinoceros's head
or an elephant's trunk
or tooth but no trace
of an animal small enough to be a belly or a woman or
womb-entrenched did you mean olden days

the number of skins

roughly 1,250,000 packed in at Hudson's Bay
as follows: Beaver Fox Lynx Marten Mink Otter
Rabbit Muskrat Bear Wolf Raccoon & Deer
or do you cite coeval sundries:
a sepulture a shrine low-lying in a riverbed chipped china

buttons or a shattered cup or trilobites
in limestone dug up for sweet does'/ my sisters' my
mother's guardian spirits long-subdued
tameless bones & trinkets & for worthless trifles
did you mean *drift*

as in portal or abundance/ a garden
spring's blandishments
& rude ornaments: Yellow Flag shimming a runoff ditch
          – in ancient Greece *kosmos* meant
everything – muck tang life & death
a single orange muddy rubber
barn glove/ hinky-fisted/ lost or thrown off in a lane
perhaps you meant prudence repurposed   *album*
graecum the dung of dogs air-whitened
          & aged for dressing leather

or stewed-in-honey curative for all what ails us
or a self-sufficient faerie province – reading Hardy
again – thrum stamen protruding or pin style prominent
          or looking away up at the Blue
-gray Gnatcatcher flitting the forest edge of my forest

          my forest
breeding or stealing food from a spider's web
or strands of weft for a tree-knot nest side
by side the softest lichen padding the purple-est
          -veined blossom-mouthed savage invader

our countryside's saint-less prayers since our country
abandons in perihelion the day when any
body in its orbit comes closest to the sun
          when the matriarchal shine
swallows our quiescence in her/ in our mother's

she is *yes*   she is relentless in her purpose
in collapse & chimera in terrene
deposits of earthen determinedly birthed in persistence
      adjacent her so-called agelessness
              her crumpling – we knew it we saw it

coming – in our greed/ our pipe dream
her paralysis – time's passing/ the calculable
disaster – in her intransigence & her diminishment
      mother *mother*   tyrant & innocent
      in the age   of drift

Dear Dearest Dear

I write pause

Reconsider/ stop retrace erase even
the *dear* too   *too*   –
start again   *here's what I mean to*   –   here's
what it –   here we go

Again **Mom** some *some* of us of us are just
just born with less skin between us
us & the nettled world the worldly world
the world's/our own passions sympathies

Imperfections this world's gloss & bighead
banter   some of us **Mom**   it's daybreak
in the park sparkle still morn here the prim pram
Oslo infants mind their sky-eyed grown-ups in the

Moment that moment of instantaneous possibility
the love predicament   *which is it?*   *less?*
more?   glacial fen or red-eddied river ***Mom***
the landscapes of childhood mark us

Forever or maybe Jack Pines & cera-muzzled
mountains are as honest-to-goodness immaterial
as mother's milk between us **Mom**   *no*
no joke   would I kid   can I can I *need*

Need   *miss*   *long for ache*   plead: *give me forgive me*
even your accusations recriminations heaven-
sent straightforward or sly I've decades ahead
to deflect absorb repent   –   redolent

Bed scents in my hindbrain   –   in this
room **Mom** the nurse's fingers bluntly not
unkindly pull the strings bare your back blooming
tang earthy recognizable as   *you*   our most

Intimate odors the essence of blood-kin you answer
yes   *yes I would*   *I need*   & all of a sudden
I've gone squeamish the thick the close *this*
close I'm nauseous **Mom** removing

Your soiled panties I cut my eyes across to your
sharp-boned hips pubis known so like
my own generous ginger patch mound mole
          – top of the right thigh –   *right*

Mom that's right I've brought fresh linens
from home   known comfort simple pleasures
not knowing now what you at least still know or
after all –   filling the blue plastic

Service pan soapy warm rivulets course my
arms run through my hands my hands
purposeful in their strategies/ immerse replenish
          squeeze twist the clean white

Cloth rust-brown bubbling
            ablution you & me in some pure
exchange   I exhale hard at the bathroom
sink begin again soft white work the inner secret

Cicatrix/ breach/ **Mom**/ your seam my hands work
their way up between your behind cleavage down
around & up & again wipe   rub   dip   wring
soothe   salve   begin   again   –

A Daughter's Aubade (sailing out from Sognefjord)

a reminiscence unremembered
a margin resurrected
an unknown though faint
as in feint
or wile/ peace of first light/ the shape of a mother

slung over my shoulder
embattled rapt
from holy lands & Baltic beaches
we were warriors in readiness
toward Ukraine's steppe we set forth unencumbered

of nonessential new
-fashioned knowledge
the percentage of nitrogen in fen or marsh
for example

or chemical compounds for coloring challis

or rare byssus silk
secreted by a gland in the foot of a pen shell
we held forth we fingered
our amber rosary beads
occluded as a cold front overtaking

a low-pressure system
on a black winter night sailing
or riding & raiding & sacking & trading

we told the faithful return
of manure to the soil

a mother's cyclical magic so plunder & shine
& shields
sweeping in from the sea
as an animal diverges two times & wanders
as I drink from a stream my fingers

pressed & cupped
enticements/ enchantments of the silk-trader's brief
& goldbeaters & metalworkers
& weavers' stories
told in scored graffiti in pediments of Hagia Sophia

I was here in short-twig runes
for the dead & dead
-still-dying brightly in etched basalt
unintentionally we carried with us mice & rats
& dung beetles

& lice & human fleas we ate remains
of pigs & sheep
& goats & cows unclean we ventured
to new world coasts & beyond the Mississippi
we left runestones

– eventually debunked –
under an aspen tree in Olof Öhman's
stubbled field & in summer season up north
in Minnesota we swam
the algal bloom in surge green

curling   *curling* wavelets top-dressed
          granite-bottomed lakes
          algae died   *dying*
fed falling basal microbes breathing
breathing
      draining oxygen from the depths
      killing native fishes & sedges
      & rivers all the way to the mounds
      of L'Anse aux Meadows
      we left cloak rings & a soapstone

spindle whorl & silver needles
          & a whetstone for sharpening whalebone scissors
a handful of iron boat nails
& jasper for sparking fire
fire & seeds

fire & seeds & sands & dust
drifted over all of these & other artifacts we dropped
in the mud
          we sailed away up the Seine & the Liffey
among a hundred others

their numbers uncounted
& prime-signed for christening we acquiesced
          in exchange for silk & damask
          robes & cloaks
& embroidered trousers from Baghdad

& just to be safe
we prayed to gods of flocks & meadows
to thunder & lightening
two moments of purity
            in spectacular confusion

& currents/ efficiencies
of size & scale pulled us on
& off & washed us clever
            but clumsy & temporary as bleeders
we opened our veins

in the various ways that mothers & daughters weep
shifting   *shifting* perceptions
of our sins' dissembling
dancing for ourselves mainly

            & for those coming up

behind from the great familial
gloom the riparian depths of the well
            for thirteen children or more
who never were
& fearless & intrepid we took out the box of family

we know so well & we thought
of grain fields' picturesque
& what occurred to us strange
as staring Marie Antoinette Marie
Antoinette Marie Antoinette angling
over/beset *beset*

praying & playing mommies & babies in the gardens
    & grandmothers'
    quavering songs their shrinking levity
& their deepest sorrow more loss
than loss can bear

burning the world tree
    that Great Ash
    at the center of the earth that feeds us all
in that moment of implied Armageddon
– a cross replaced to show who's

who – who's in charge

    as the culling of a wolf trees
marks clash & asylum
    & exposure ineffable as harmony
    or hatred

we looked to chimpanzees to cage-tested
experiments caged & sweating out
mercury like saliva the day we read
    the results looking into each other's eyes
    & I said

    you take no prisoners   *ever mother*

ever mothered on sacred pilgrimage mother
vessel mother of small
    & slender aspect but Jesus   *Jesus*
    you stoic you hard-ass

you Viking scoured & saved
your womanly remains: a hank of hair a fingernail's
    fragment fiercely guarded
    you sibyl birthed three siblings
made of brutal siege   on holiday

we climbed the impotent hillsides
we let ourselves in at the farmyard gate
knocked at the red-painted cottage door in search
    of our lost race
    speaking a language

that couldn't be heard
    we grand-mothered mothered
grand-daughtered/ scanned plateaus & skies for signs
for manifestations of strength
& weakness in maternal peaks'

reflections in Sognefjord's depth   & thrall
    recaptured together sooner or later in
dawn's scald harnessed   we set sail
    yesterday
    or twelve-hundred years ago   today

Crone

I slipped looking up
& all the hounds of hell
          yawned & turned their backs
let us go track

& trail/ thoroughfare/ traversing our hard-headed
          trajectory
dicey victories   logistics hid

under fat moil   a cloak a rill/ a clasp
          mother
pitted in coral cabochon/ pulverized
in limestone/ chapter

& verse/ marble dust troweled to perfection/ your hips
my thighs your beautiful shoulders
          my rounded alfresco   rubbed

to luster   mother   now gristly
          in infirmity I reckon indignities
as sufferance/ fancy plaster effigies

          as a child's curled hands
covering lips/ pupae/ golden
butterflies alight in tandem   aflutter

from my mouth stuffed with dressmaker's pins
          mother   mother
your eyes
          crackerjack squint as shark back then

I'd squat waiting
    at the metal grate
admiring Spring's fat lambs/ your sharp slaughter tools

    you'd take your sweet time as though
all your accumulated riches
    addled & alms   a whip so snap

so break-neck curt slit me open mid-brow
    to the bone
I've counted up the lessons in love's arctic
cortège

    totaled up the traces
    my/your/our body parts

in evidence: I don't amount to too much anymore
but then   *then*   hallowed be   *hallowed*

    I was jejune & ancient/ she-demon's
fever
amateur porn flick   still
no prize-winner for piety
you'd forth-come cursorily give out ill-advisedly
I'd take seconds or thirds/ a fourth helping
    on a bender   a jag   antic you'd say
give me   *get me*   *sharp as satrap*
    cold as a crone

On Winning the Marathon at Sixty

As if there were fireflies awake at dawn
As though the bite of frost on grass

were fastened to the leaked night
the sneaked light

as if trepidation wore the bib
not the runner

as though the runner rode sweetness in anticipation
as the colors of slate & water & the washing over

of flat river stones smoothed the size & shape
of a Red Hawk tail feather

the blue-gray-black wind catch/ my gloves tucked
into my singlet

quick stripping to shorts at the first water stop as if
this journey recalls the end   yet not

& exhaustion is the sweetest of all
my body's immunological betrayals

as though condition/ disease/ sickliness
is one fewer fugitive   as if to walk yet not

as if pain is anything/everything
of pleasure   as if illness as if tenderness & toughness

ruthlessness stricken in delicacy
in the doe's white tail flying boundless as if

ransomed by this run to the start line
& color corrals & sweetness of all in the crossing

in the final mile: I want to start again   *right now*
in attenuation/ time's compaction   as though a quiff

of air led/ barely contained   *I'm lit*
watching the clock at each turn

if in the reach as in the grasp   the enveloping
as though in the use of every muscle bone bit of cracking

cartilage: the floating & rafting on
everything   legs light   up on my toes to the end

in the atavistic hour

of course the flocks know where to fly & what to do
with their spindly legs between silence

& the world's white bones post -
shorn/ wool scorch/ in sun's first blush   in our still
slumber   a pink blink   an orange swell

in luxury in extremity's

transcendence in the atavistic hour the hour post
-blizzard in ignorance in threat & tenderness
in our old habit's slow golden

smile in the purgatorial blaze/ numb fingers & toes
immersed

in the inheritor's hot memory/ shivery/ a diapered child
toddles out/ a skating figure drifts &
stumbles/ stirruped

in arctic whorls & blanched stalks
plumed prairie
our errors & perfections   our
birthright snow-blind

etched/ icy   in opalescent crust

vi. Trillium erectum/ Wake Robin

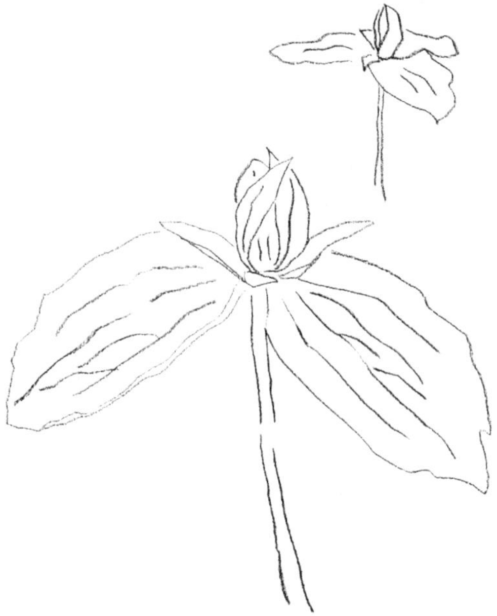

I could live brief but calm sans
goals or decisions or opportunities or realizations
or failures or successes or duties

obligations
ephemeral

Spring's a flicker-shine
Flesh Flies' sojourn
wake-robin foul

blossom's rot meat scent I could sly spread
my rhizomes clandestine
pretending at forevers

Foxhole

i.

& if I could tell you anything I would say
good fortune & the promise of tomorrow
don't come easy   I would say
find a foxhole   always expect the worst & if it
comes
you're ready   meanwhile

on another kind of battleground in a different war
I fight darkness but hide in its current behind
the coated whitewash of those who know what's best
for me in mutations that petrify me

– I know illness my legs won't hold –

bumping down Pine Street in a cart
careering between lockdown & horde
resentment in this great dismal swamp of the only habits
we think we can live with

& if I could tell you I would say *nobody ever promised you*
anything   meanwhile

in cities' mourning & commemorations among
uniformed gunmen there are always a hundred
walls of separation
so the office ladies tell it growing up
at the margin/ military at their throats bawling out

identity cards & where're

you from
I'm from America/ listening
hard to subtleties of accent & the unsaid/ blunt fingered
        & sleepless/ submerged in glitter-skid
        dislocation feeling around jetlag
        for any kind of custom I can

ii.

        & the Irish ladies say they dread the hardening
of the border – again – or any border where bouquets
painted on walls mark equivalents
        of funeral flowers & the sea
        becomes the checkpoint
for the fragility of any peace/ can of worms
        in calmer times/   oh never mind/   bollocks

no surer then riding along on children's
handlebars & 31 miles from the border they're holding
on to weapons in the attic – the ladies say – just in case
        it all comes back around   *just in case*
& you know
        they're selling more guns

than ever & it's not just
to preppers in the Land of Liberty
& if I could tell you anything I would say
        good fortune & the promise of tomorrow
        don't come easy   I would say
bunker down   so when it comes

        when it

iii.

meanwhile I'm listening to morning rain birds
sing to high heaven in scorched summer fields
of long *long* days

& short solstice nights & if you're still with me
I would add *get used to it* *toughen up*

you can stand more than you know

ambit of absence

grace shapes the white the isolation the incised
of crystalline miniatures/ ice-heaved
sidewalks & the millionth fallen ginkgo
leaf before the flurry/ the amassment/ golden folded
packets smashed pasty/ reminiscence's tender
spice leftover in the breath the moan the ambit
of absence *we're barely*
there our pasts carved up
in fools' errands/ sincerely/ our one-dog-night
chase over frozen crags & strands the inevitable
& destructible the puny gray-furred lying thing
encountered bloody-muzzled bushy hind
-legged blank baby blind-eyed *thing* leaping
back to life/ wily trickster shapeshifter *but no*
no poise no polish spans us buck naked waving
our arms & legs marking angels
in breadcrumbs or crawling
through a snow fort's nave fur-collared/ burrowed
wrapped in childhood's strange
descant our cotter strain legendary
& brooding – seeing the pond's bottom
through the ice for what it is – for grace
licking our wounds safely after unholy harsh's
had its way – our upland's full blossoming
after abeyance between
mystic & intolerable
solitude when solitude won't save us & language
fails us in the intermittent
light from the snowplow riffling our pre-dawn
windows/ snow shroud/ the simplest/ the scouring
sensation of where we've been &
where we are

Reap

What stratagem or mystery
    an image scraped from wax lees
bird-blood warmed encaustic   fettered
a mouse's spine crushed by incisors embedded

Sticky

In a child a woman the wanderer's seed of flight
what we receive & continue to receive
by fires of blessing & burgeon by smoke

    & flame rising
above the scrubbed pine & spindly sapling fields
in new growth   in riddle & dream-thrill

    I bothered to look for you

Among the Redbud's nub-budded branches' bruised
    nuclei/ healing pear & plum
in bog-ore raked for smelting
in glacial gravel& stones repudiating the plow

    I looked for you in metal alloys

Bronze or brass   nickel or pewter
your hair cinched in nets of unrecalled or past
    recollection

In the roe's eye   blossoming/ rent visions
    of movement & passage

rudiment & essence – if immateriality is the home of
God –

I puzzled over kindnesses & thank-offerings wrapped
          in other animals' furs/ extremity's passing
fondling a figurine   carried *carried*

          I looked for you

As a leather-strung amulet   a fetish stretched
          round my neck as a souvenir
of the little we know of residence

          or relic of permanence

Or rampant – our pagan amplitude – our tools
of acquiescence – en pathos – in sweet reap fierce
          & final

Lazarus Weed Belief

The emerald ash borer, an invasive insect species thought
to have arrived in shipping containers, in two decades has
decimated billions of ash trees throughout North America.

casualty embodies the gift call it rook
or swindle that summer's scorch that hundredth
summit our margin the piedmont between dry
west & humid east call it susceptivity & indemnity
the centenary meridian/ our sob story
even before we sniffed the Sweetbay's goblet
blossomings/ our canicular days' chill & hot weak-
kneed nights/ our Lazarus weed belief even
when discovery came late our penalty a modern
contagion crawling out from a shipping container
scarcity to exotic plague sliding down the marsh
to dusty shingle I remember other landscapes

lying flat out we looked

straight up at the sky/ stripped & snooped & sniffed
an abandoned sauna's desiccant sweat/ oblate
we thought we saw grace-profiled saints in our arbor
we never looked for decay in the ash
outside our window/ we saw verve
& sparkling sprung & never noticed
the pileated woodpeckers
digging for larvae – there's always some invader
some – driving numberless holes in the bark

not walking away we peered up into the crown
as lost leaves collected at our feet
collapsing the canopy in dieback/ the flume

of illness's vertigo of time & distance compressed
in furnace bloom: ruinous toll & ill-starred upshot
official & hot from the mouth
of some local Master Gardener
thus we called a truce for time/ guessed
the unofficial armistice might yet
steel us with strategies/ panaceæ/ our adversaries
thereby made indifferently strong & savage
yet on the skids our faith rose from ruin
we believed in the trinity of *our* & *us*
in holding out though not a prayer held out
the possibility of revival/ recovery
– in half-knowledge bliss –   & the gelding
followed contingent on the blow-by-blow unholy

tunneling in bright metallic gasps/ in the terrifying
competence of acetic insects S-shuddering
our babies' cambia   amoebas burrowed
deep in their bodies' cavities   yet we disbelieved
the degree-day computation & wept the war
sans embarrassment/ that's all we could do
in our stand-down in parasitic seizure
as any sufferer incarnates the gift   call it
argument or proof/ decline or détente
our sweet ashes leafless/ denuded/ made small
in that measure   to which in time
we acquiesced

Arillus

For ungulates' baby martyrs/ tiny fawns'
hayfield release/ plained world *llaneros:*
sickle bar & baling
twine –

And for me: pine near-toppled boughs
ringed & ridged in a fog that never
lifts –

For shimmying my old conterminous ass
testy narrow scarlet-cockled petals' floor –
fallen calyces &

For summer storm-bruised cerecloth
gasp to midden a lanyard a ream a stroke
flushed as fever – For

Tremens jerk/ a park in a Latin American city
refrigerator boxes'
leathery eaves – for sexing the solitary

The arbitrary for companionless or bound twos
or threes in roguery at branches' ends –
For insects inseminate increase:

Two dragonflies alight one atop
another lavaliered boogied-out on sun-
burnt flesh/ my little boat floating

Fast & free adrift/ smooth timbre-d limbs
two against all comers combined –
For tippy-tongued muscles'

Meticulous lists: mark not nor number
but hasten *hasten* – For musician's
Cuatro terrestrial *joropo*: a kind of people's

Waltz *mi corazón* indiscriminate
couplings membranous spongy-pulp bitter
tissue fruit set yield covert mortifications

Syncopations fancy my body's
a featherless bed – For plaster-cast
damp wrinkled
sweat

For dew beads' dimmed glits for split
unembarrassed gross & sweet & acidy juicy-
reddy – Or whitish

Arillus:

An outgrowth a covering – For mace
to nutmeg spice to savor in each sac
a single an angular a hard a soft

seed.

vii. Cow Lily Coda

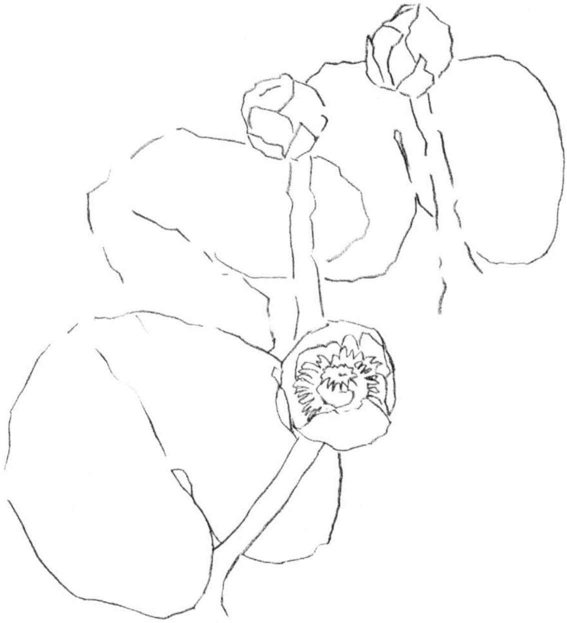

for fallacy: symbiosis vs. illusion
a means to an end/ a suggested elixir
the cure for excessive cravings

vitae: from the lower parts to the heart
& the throat's expression   outflanking ardor
for torments & spasms   for my agitation:
two as one/ I got to get me   *some*

for the skirmish: the blink returned as remedy
& antidote & take the road   back home

Flora/ Native Plants Index

1

Pontederia cordata or Pickerelweed is a vigorous aquatic perennial native to the American continent. It flourishes in quiet wetlands, marshes, streams and lake margins. Nectar-feeding insects visit the flowers, submerged stems and leaves provide refuge for a variety of animals.

15

Antennaria plantaginifolia or Pussy Toes, and also known as Woman's Tobacco, is a small tender spring-blooming forb with wooly white flower heads and downy basal leaves. It is native east of the Mississippi and prefers rocky roadsides and dry sandy slopes.

29

Monarda didyma or American Beebalm, an aromatic herb native to the central and eastern United States, grows exuberantly along the margins of rills, ditches, and streams. It thrives in sunny locations with well-drained soil. Its lush red flowers attract hummingbirds.

45

Sarracenia purpurea or Purple Pitcher Plant, is a carnivorous perennial, the only one of its genus to inhabit colder temperate climates including the Gulf Coast and the Eastern seaboard of the

United States. Prey fall into the pitcher, drowning in rainwater collected in each bulbous basal leaf.

59

Symplocarpus foetidus or Skunk Cabbage, is early spring-flowering & found growing in wetlands areas emerging from frozen mud; a thermogenetic plant, it can generate temperatures that melt ice. It's heat-producing properties and foul odor attract carrion-feeding insects to the spathe for pollination.

79

Trillium erectum or Wake Robin, is a spring ephemeral native to the Eastern United States; its three-petaled flowers are a deep red color. Trillium tolerates extremely harsh temperatures, it's brief life cycle synchronized with the damp deciduous forests where it flourishes. The leaves of the plant are poisonous.

91

Nuphar advena or Cow Lily is native throughout the eastern United States and is found in ponds and sluggish streams, its leaves lying heavily on the surface and its bright yellow cupped and bulbous blooms emerging above the waterline. Native American people reportedly used the plant medicinally, for example for treating heart ailments, but large doses of the powdered root may be toxic.

Acknowledgements

New Southerner, online publication, summer 2019:
the menisci of tenderness

The Poetry Anthology 2021 Volume 1, The Cuddy Family Foundation for Veterans: *Sfumato*

Stony Thursday Poetry Book 2017, Limerick Culture and Arts Office, Ireland: *Purple Spear Thistle*

Rumble Fish, Winter 2019: *in solstice*

Acumen Issue 102, Winter 2022: *Drawing the Sacred Dog*

Winchester Poetry Prize Winners Anthology, The Blaze in Father's Breath, 2018:
a birder's cacophony/ kettle lake & moraine

Dogwood: A Journal of Poetry & Prose, Dogwood Literary Awards issue, Spring 2018:
Imago & the Io Moth

Diode Editions Wrecked Archive Anthology 2022:
Balsam/ sister sister

Off the Coast, Fall 2016 vol. 2: *Anamnesis*

Tupelo Press 2018, Tupelo Quarterly 16, Collaborations & Cross-disciplinary Texts:
Monarda didyma/ American Beebalm

Mississippi Review, No. 46, 2018 Prize Issue: *Milfoil*

Rabble Review, Issue No. 2, 2022: *Judas Hole*; *Taproot*

Talking Writing (digital journal), Winter 2019: *Reliquiae Flyway*

Crosswinds Poetry Journal, Spring 2017: *Mine*

Back from the Brink, *We are a many-bodied singing thing,* Speculative fiction and poetry inspired by endangered species and the people saving them, U.K., 2020: *The Trackers Tale*

Marsh Hawk Review, Fall 2018: *after Corot in love*

Comstock Review 30th Anniversary Issue, 2016: *River*

Middle Creek Publishing Fledge Chapbook Competition Winner 2018: *A Daughter's Aubade, (sailing out from Sognefjord); Crone*

University of Canterbury Festival Prize Anthology 2016: *Dear Dearest Dear;The Sea Between Us*

Mslexia Journal Showcase Issue 91, Fall 2021: *Age of Drift*

The Poetry Business/ Smith Doorstop Press Running Anthology 2019: *The Result Is What You See Today*, *On Winning the Marathon at Sixty*

Crossroads Review, Spring 2018: *in the atavistic hour*

Erbacce-press Journal, Winter 2019: *Reap*

National Poetry Society Competition 2015 Commended Poem, website publication: *Arillus*

About the Author

Mara Adamitz Scrupe is a visual artist, writer and documentary filmmaker and the recipient of many creative grants and fellowships. Her cross-disciplinary creative practice explores a terrain of psychic, emotional and physical kinship with nature; her installations, artist books, sculptures, drawings, poems, and essays investigate how we as thinking animals are shaped and changed – emotionally, socially, politically, and spiritually – by our interdependencies with the natural world. Mara is the author of six prizewinning poetry collections, and she has won or been shortlisted for prestigious international writing prizes including National Poetry Society Competition (UK) and Aesthetica Poetry Prize (UK). She serves concurrently as Lance Williams Resident Artist in the Arts & Sciences, University of Kansas/ Lawrence, and Dean and Professor Emerita, School of Art, University of the Arts, Philadelphia. Mara lives with her husband on their farm bordering the James River in the Blue Ridge Piedmont countryside of central Virginia.

Made in the USA
Monee, IL
20 March 2023

30068102R00069